MODERN IRISH FOOD

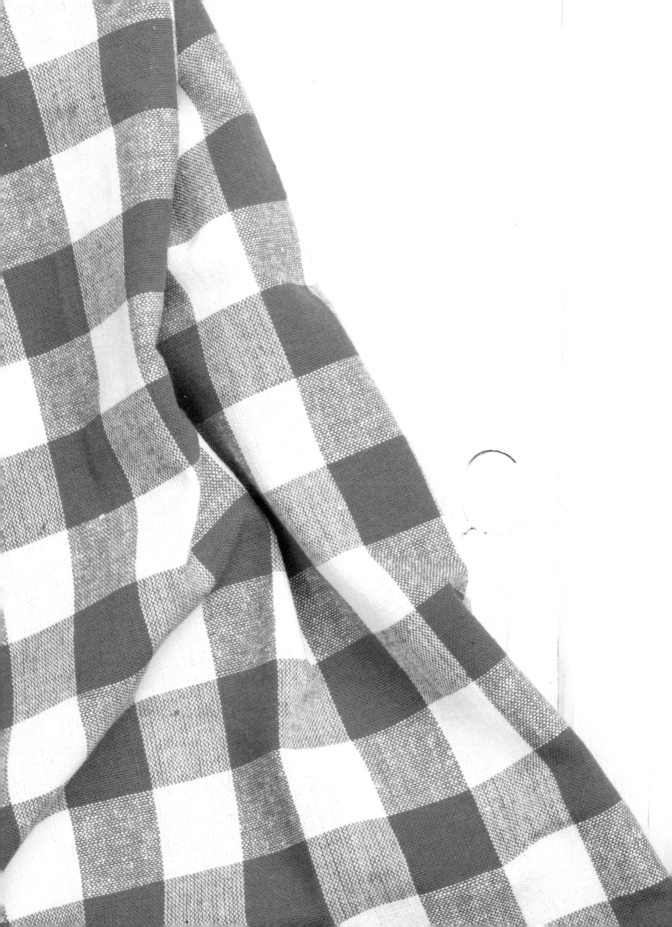

MODERN IRISH FOOD

Traditional tastes with modern flavour

Bounty Books

Modern Irish Food

Publisher: Samantha Warrington
Editor: Phoebe Morgan
Production Controller: Sarah Kramer
Project Editor: Jane Birch
Designer: Chris Bell/cbdesign

Published in 2016 by Bounty Books,
a division of Octopus Publishing Group Ltd
Carmelite House
50 Victoria Embankment
London, EC4Y 0DZ
www.octopusbooks.co.uk

An Hachette UK Company
www.hachette.co.uk

ISBN: 978-0-753730-07-2

Printed and bound in China

CONTENTS

INTRODUCTION

IN IRELAND, THE KITCHEN HAS ALWAYS BEEN – AND REMAINS today – the heart of the home. While Irish food retains many of its roots, modern Irish cooks and chefs are incorporating ideas, ingredients and flavours from other parts of the world with the best of traditional cuisine to create food that is as delicious as it is innovative.

Contemporary Irish cooking is steeped in a rich heritage and draws on the wealth of ingredients available from the sea and the land, including:

POTATOES

Ireland's national vegetable, the potato arrived in Ireland in the second half of 16th century and rapidly became a staple food crop. The high mineral and vitamin content made it the perfect, cheap food for the poor. The dependence on potatoes was to be a curse, with the Potato Famine of 1845–49 wiping out potato crops and resulting in the deaths of around a million people. A million more people were forced to emigrate.

Today the potato is still a major feature of Irish cuisine in favourite traditional dishes such as colcannon and champ, and potatoes remain key to Irish cooking, used in new and delicious ways, such as Potato & Smoked Garlic Soup (see page 10), Pumpkin, Leek & Potato Bake (see page 39), Smoked Mackerel & New Potato Salad (see page 29) and Bacon, Thyme & Potato Muffins (see page 125).

FISH AND SEAFOOD

Ireland's clean, unpolluted Atlantic coasts are rich in seafood and fish, which have always formed a vital part of the daily diet. Today Irish fish and seafood – including salmon, trout, herring, mackerel, mussels, oysters and scallops – are widely eaten at home and are also exported.

MEAT

Lamb, pork and beef have always been a part of Irish eating, featuring in famous traditional dishes such as Irish stew, and they are still important today. This book has some great contemporary takes on traditional meat-based meals including Spiced Cabbage & Bacon Pan-fry (see page 77) and Rosemary-crusted Roast Lamb (page 67).

CHEESE

The artisan cheese industry has grown dramatically since the 1970s, with the increased demand for top-quality cheeses and now Ireland has over 120 different cheese types from strong, sharp Cheddars to Cashel Blue, which was the first Irish blue cheese.

FRUITS AND VEGETABLES

Like Irish cooks of the past, contemporary Irish cooks makes the most of fresh fruits and vegetables – ranging from traditional favourites like apples, pears, kale, carrots and cabbage to rediscovered foraged ingredients, including samphire, nettles and elderflowers.

BEER, WHISKEY AND CIDER

With its characteristic taste and distinctive appearance, Ireland's internationally famous and most widely consumed alcoholic beverage is Guinness. Cider-making stretches back at least 2,000 years with religious orders and monasteries making it alongside beer throughout Ireland. Today, craft cider-making is enjoying a revival in Ireland. Also experiencing a resurgence of popularity worldwide is Irish whiskey. Several recipes in this book use a drop of Ireland's favourite tipples, including Beef, Pickled Onion & Guinness Stew (see page 71), Cider & Chicken Pie (see page 86) and Irish Whiskey Syllabub (see page 109).

FOOD FESTIVALS

There is always an excuse to celebrate food and drink in Ireland and each year sees a plethora of festivals both large and small – focusing on everything from beer and potatoes to apples and fish – held the length and breadth of Ireland. Among them are The Galway International Oyster Festival, which has been held annually since 1954 and features a wide range of oyster-based dishes, The Roscommon Lamb Festival, celebrating the importance of lamb in the Irish diet, and Taste of Dublin, which is a gastronomic extravaganza focusing on Irish food and restaurants.

WHETHER HEARTY POTATO-BASED RECIPES OR DELICATELY

flavoured with summer herbs, soups in Ireland have always

been made with simple, seasonal ingredients and provide a

tempting starter or a satisfying meal in themselves.

SOUPS

POTATO & SMOKED GARLIC SOUP

Serves 4
Preparation time 10–15 minutes
Cooking time 30–35 minutes

50 g (2 oz) unsalted butter
1 large onion, sliced
2 smoked garlic cloves, crushed
750 g (1½ lb) floury potatoes,
   peeled and cut into small cubes

1 litre (1¾ pints) vegetable stock
½ teaspoon smoked sea salt
125 ml (4 fl oz) milk
4 tablespoons fresh herbs,
   such as parsley, thyme and
   chives, plus extra snipped
   chives to garnish
pepper
Greek yogurt, to serve

Melt the butter in a large saucepan, add the onion and smoked garlic and cook over a medium heat for 3–4 minutes until softened. Stir in the potatoes, cover and cook for 5 minutes.

Add the stock and season with the smoked sea salt and pepper. Bring to the boil, then reduce the heat, cover and simmer for 30 minutes until the potatoes are tender.

Transfer to a food processor or blender, in batches, and blend until smooth. Return to the pan, stir in the milk and herbs and reheat gently.

Serve in bowls with a spoonful of Greek yogurt, garnished with chives and freshly ground pepper.

Makes a delicious winter supper

CREAM OF LEEK & PEA SOUP

Serves 6
Preparation time 15 minutes
Cooking time 20 minutes

2 tablespoons olive oil
375 g (12 oz) leeks, trimmed,
  cleaned and thinly sliced
375 g (12 oz) fresh or frozen peas

small bunch mint
900 ml (1½ pints) vegetable
  or chicken stock
150 g (5 oz) mascarpone cheese
grated rind of 1 small lemon
salt and pepper
mint leaves, to garnish

Heat the oil in a saucepan, add the leeks, toss in the oil then cover and fry gently for 10 minutes, stirring occasionally, until softened but not coloured. Mix in the peas and cook briefly.

Pour the stock into the pan, add a little salt and pepper then bring to the boil. Cover and simmer gently for 10 minutes.

Ladle half the soup into a blender or food processor, add all the mint and blend until smooth. Pour the purée back into the saucepan. Mix the mascarpone with half of the lemon rind, reserving the rest for a garnish. Spoon half the mixture into the soup, then reheat, stirring until the mascarpone has melted. Taste and adjust the seasoning if needed.

Ladle the soup into bowls, top with spoonfuls of the remaining mascarpone and a sprinkling of the remaining lemon rind. Garnish with mint leaves.

MUSSEL SOUP WITH SAFFRON & GARLIC

Serves 4–6
Preparation time 30 minutes
Cooking time 25 minutes

30–40 fresh mussels,
    approximately 1.5 kg (3 lb)
75 g (3 oz) butter
1 onion, finely sliced
175 g (6 oz) leeks, white part only,
    trimmed, cleaned and finely
    sliced
1 bouquet garni
125 ml (4 fl oz) dry white wine
2 garlic cloves, crushed
175 g (6 oz) carrots, finely chopped
1 celery stick, finely sliced
750 ml (1¼ pints) fish stock
pinch of saffron
150 ml (¼ pint) double cream
salt and pepper
chervil fronds, to garnish
    (optional)

To prepare the mussels, wash them under cold running water and scrape, removing the beard (the hairy attachment protruding from the mussel) and any barnacles attached to the shells. Discard any mussels that are open or damaged.

Heat 25 g (1 oz) of the butter in a very large saucepan, add one-third of the onion and leek and cook over a gentle heat until soft. Add the mussels, bouquet garni and wine. Cover and cook over a high heat for 4–5 minutes, stirring occasionally.

When all the mussel shells have opened, drain through a piece of muslin lining a sieve set over a bowl to catch the cooking juices. Set the reserved cooking juices aside. Remove the mussels from their shells, discarding any that haven't opened. Refrigerate until needed.

Heat the remaining butter to the saucepan and gently fry the garlic, carrots and celery until soft. Add the fish stock and reserved mussel juices. Add the mussels, reserving 12 to garnish the soup. Bring to the boil and cook gently for 20 minutes. Add the saffron, stir in the cream and purée in a blender or food processor until smooth.

Return to the pan, season to taste, stir in the whole mussels and slowly reheat. Serve immediately garnished with chervil fronds, if liked.

POTATO, APPLE & LEEK SOUP

Serves 4
Preparation time 10 minutes
Cooking time 25 minutes

25 g (1 oz) butter
1 tablespoon sunflower oil
450 g (1 lb) leeks, trimmed,
  cleaned and sliced

2 potatoes, peeled and diced
2 dessert apples, peeled, cored
  and diced
150 ml (¼ pint) dry cider
900 ml (1½ pints) vegetable
  stock
salt and pepper
grated Gruyère cheese, to serve

Melt the butter with the oil in a large saucepan over a medium heat, add the leeks and cook for 5 minutes until starting to soften.

Stir the potatoes and apples into the pan, cover and cook for a further 5 minutes.

Add the cider and cook, uncovered, until reduced by half. Stir in the stock, cover and simmer for 15 minutes until the potatoes are tender. Serve topped with grated Gruyère cheese.

Serve with chunks of warm, crusty bread

PEA, POTATO & ROCKET SOUP

Serves 4–6
Preparation time 15 minutes
Cooking time 35 minutes

3 tablespoons extra virgin olive oil,
   plus extra to serve
1 onion, finely chopped
2 garlic cloves, finely chopped

2 teaspoons chopped thyme
250 g (8 oz) potatoes, chopped
500 g (1 lb) frozen or fresh peas
1 litre (1¾ pints) vegetable stock
100 g (3½ oz) rocket leaves,
   roughly chopped
juice of 1 lemon
salt and pepper

Heat the oil in a saucepan, add the onion, garlic and thyme and cook over a low heat, stirring frequently, for 5 minutes until the onion is softened. Add the potatoes and cook, stirring frequently, for 5 minutes.

Stir in the peas, stock and salt and pepper. Bring to the boil, then reduce the heat, cover and simmer gently for 20 minutes.

Transfer the soup to a food processor or blender, add the rocket and lemon juice and process until smooth. Return to the pan, adjust the seasoning and heat through. Serve immediately, drizzled with a little extra oil.

BUTTER BEAN & BACON SOUP

Serves 4
Preparation time 15 minutes
Cooking time 25 minutes

2 tablespoons olive oil
175 g (6 oz) smoked bacon, chopped
25 g (1 oz) butter
1 onion, chopped
2 garlic cloves, roughly chopped
2 celery sticks, chopped

1 leek, roughly chopped
750 ml (1¼ pints) hot ham or vegetable stock
400 g (13 oz) can butter beans, drained and rinsed
2 large sprigs of parsley
3 sprigs of thyme
2 bay leaves
100 ml (3½ fl oz) double cream
salt and pepper

Heat 1 tablespoon of the oil in a large pan and fry the bacon until it is crisp and golden. Remove with a slotted spoon and set aside to drain on kitchen paper.

Melt the butter and remaining oil in the pan over a medium heat and cook the onion, garlic, celery and leek, stirring frequently, for about 10 minutes or until soft and golden.

Add the stock and butter beans with the herbs and season to taste. Bring to the boil, then turn the heat down and simmer gently for about 10 minutes before removing from the heat. Remove the herbs and blend until smooth.

Stir in the cream, season to taste and serve in bowls, scattered with pieces of crispy bacon.

A real winter warmer...

KALE SOUP WITH GARLIC CROUTONS

Serves 8
Preparation time 25 minutes
Cooking time 45 minutes

50 g (2 oz) butter
1 onion, chopped
2 carrots, sliced
500 g (1 lb) kale, tough stalks
   discarded
1.2 litres (2 pints) water
600 ml (1 pint) vegetable stock
1 tablespoon lemon juice

300 g (10 oz) potatoes, sliced
pinch of grated nutmeg
salt and pepper
2 kale leaves, thinly shredded,
   to garnish

garlic croutons
90–125 ml (3½–4 fl oz) olive oil
3 garlic cloves, sliced
6–8 slices wholemeal bread, crusts
   removed, cut into 1 cm (½ inch)
   cubes

Melt the butter in a large saucepan, add the onion and cook over a medium heat for 5 minutes or until soft. Add the carrots and kale in batches, stirring constantly. Cook for 2 minutes until the kale has just wilted.

Pour in the measurement water and stock, then add the lemon juice, potatoes and nutmeg. Season with salt and pepper. Bring to the boil, then reduce the heat, cover and simmer for 30–35 minutes until all the vegetables are tender. Add a little water if the soup is too thick.

Make the croutons while the soup is cooking. Heat the oil in a large frying pan, add the garlic and cook over a medium heat for 1 minute. Add the bread cubes and cook, turning frequently, until golden brown. Remove with a slotted spoon and drain on kitchen paper. Remove and discard the garlic. Add the shredded kale to the pan and cook, stirring constantly, until crispy.

Reheat the soup gently. Serve in bowls, garnished with the croutons and crispy shredded kale.

MODERN IRISH COOKING TAKES THE BOUNTY THE EMERALD

Isle offers and showcases it in fresh dishes that includes crisp, flavourful salads made with ingredients such as locally produced cheeses and delicious smoked fish.

SALADS & LIGHT MEALS

APPLE, CASHEL BLUE & NUT SALAD

Serves 4
Preparation time 15 minutes +
   cooling time
Cooking time 10 minutes

15 g (½ oz) unsalted butter
2 tablespoons caster sugar
2 red dessert apples, cored and
   cut into thin wedges
75 g (3 oz) walnut pieces

½ small red cabbage, thinly sliced
2 celery sticks, chopped
150 g (5 oz) Cashel Blue cheese,
   crumbled

dressing
2 tablespoons walnut oil
2 tablespoons olive oil
2 tablespoons balsamic vinegar
salt and pepper

Melt the butter in a frying pan, add the sugar and stir over a low heat until the sugar has dissolved.

Add the apples to the pan and cook for 3–4 minutes on each side until they start to caramelize, then stir in the walnuts and cook for 1 minute. Remove from the heat and leave to cool.

Place the red cabbage and celery in a bowl, then add the cooled apple and walnut mixture.

Make the dressing. Place the oils and vinegar in a screw-top jar with salt and pepper to taste, add the lid and shake well.

Drizzle the dressing over the ingredients in the bowl and toss together. Serve immediately, scattered with the Cashel Blue cheese.

SMOKED TROUT, CUCUMBER & RADISH SALAD

Serves 4
Preparation time 10 minutes

2 tablespoons mayonnaise
2 tablespoons fromage frais
lemon juice, to taste
125 g (4 oz) skinless smoked trout
   fillets, broken into large flakes
½ cucumber, sliced
6 radishes, thinly sliced
50 g (2 oz) watercress
pepper
toasted soda bread, to serve

Mix together the mayonnaise and fromage frais with lemon juice to taste and season well with pepper.

Arrange the trout, cucumber, radishes and watercress on a serving plates. Drizzle over the mayonnaise mixture and serve with plenty of toasted soda bread.

A healthy summer lunch

SMOKED MACKEREL
& NEW POTATO SALAD

Serves 4
Preparation time 10 minutes
Cooking time 15 minutes

750 g (1½ lb) new potatoes, halved
  if large
200 g (7 oz) crème fraîche
2 teaspoons creamed horseradish

juice of 1 lemon
2 tablespoons pumpkin seeds
4 smoked mackerel fillets, about
  100 g (3½ oz) each, skinned
  and flaked
175 g (6 oz) watercress
salt and pepper

Cook the potatoes in a saucepan of boiling water for 15–16 minutes until tender.

Meanwhile, mix together the crème fraîche, horseradish and lemon juice in a large serving bowl and season to taste.

Heat a nonstick frying pan over a medium-low heat and dry-fry the pumpkin seeds for 2–3 minutes, stirring frequently, until golden brown and toasted. Set aside.

Drain the potatoes, then refresh under cold running water and drain again. Mix with the crème fraîche mixture. Gently toss in the mackerel and watercress.

Serve sprinkled with the toasted pumpkin seeds.

POTTED CRAB & PRAWNS

Crabs and other shellfish were once gathered by Irish coastal dwellers as their main source of protein. They are still a much enjoyed feature of Irish cuisine.

Serves 4
Preparation time 25 minutes
  + chilling time
Cooking time 10 minutes

200 g (7 oz) butter, diced
finely grated rind and juice of
  1 lime
3 tablespoons chopped coriander
generous pinch of cayenne pepper

200 g (7 oz) peeled, cooked
  prawns, roughly chopped
1 dressed crab, about 175 g (6 oz)
salt

to serve
½ small wholemeal baguette,
  sliced
2 heads of chicory
a few tiny radishes

First clarify the butter. Heat a small saucepan of water, add the butter and heat gently until melted. Cool, then freeze until the butter has formed a set layer on top of the water. Lift the disc of hardened butter off the water and discard the water. Remove any droplets of water from the underside of the butter with kitchen paper.

Melt half the clarified butter in a saucepan. Add the lime rind, chopped coriander, cayenne and a little salt. Stir the prawns into the butter with the crab meat and lime juice. Heat until piping hot. Spoon into 4 small china ramekins and press down well so there are no air pockets. Chill for 15 minutes.

Melt the remaining butter in a clean pan then spoon over the top of the fish mixture in a thin even layer. Chill for 3–4 hours until set. Sprinkle with a little extra cayenne.

Toast the bread then arrange on plates with the dishes of potted fish. Serve with chicory leaves and tiny radishes.

POTATO & BACON CAKES

Serves 4
Preparation time 15 minutes +
  chilling time
Cooking time 40–45 minutes

1 kg (2 lb) potatoes, cut into
  chunks
vegetable oil, for shallow-frying
6 spring onions, sliced
200 g (7 oz) back bacon, chopped

2 tablespoons chopped flat leaf
  parsley
plain flour, for coating
25 g (1 oz) butter
salt and pepper

tomato sauce
200 ml (7 fl oz) crème fraîche
2 tablespoons chopped basil
2 tablespoons chopped tomatoes

Cook the potatoes in a large saucepan of salted boiling water for 15–20 minutes until tender. Drain well, return to the pan and mash.

Heat a little oil in a frying pan, add the spring onions and cook for 2–3 minutes, then add the bacon and cook until browned. Add to the mash with the parsley. Season well with salt and pepper. Form the potato mixture into 8 cakes, then cover and chill in the refrigerator until firm.

Lightly coat the cakes in flour. Melt the butter in a nonstick frying pan, add the cakes, in batches, and cook over a medium heat for 4–5 minutes on each side until browned and heated through.

Meanwhile, to make the sauce, put the crème fraîche in a bowl and mix in the basil and tomatoes. Season well with salt and pepper.

Serve the cakes hot with the sauce.

ONION, WALNUT & CASHEL BLUE CHEESE TARTS

Serves 4
Preparation time 20 minutes
  + cooling time
Cooking time 35–40 minutes

40 g (1½ oz) butter
500 g (1 lb) onions, thinly sliced
2 garlic cloves, crushed

1 tablespoon chopped thyme
50 g (2 oz) walnuts, chopped
350 g (11½ oz) puff pastry,
  defrosted if frozen
plain flour, for dusting
150 g (5 oz) Cashel Blue cheese,
  diced
salt and pepper

Melt the butter in a frying pan, add the onions, garlic and thyme and cook over a medium heat, stirring occasionally, for 20–25 minutes until soft and golden. Stir in the walnuts. Leave to cool.

Roll the pastry out on a lightly floured work surface to form a rectangle 40 x 20 cm (16 x 8 inches), trimming the edges. Cut the rectangle vertically in half, then cut horizontally into quarters to make eight 10 cm (4 inch) squares.

Divide the onion mixture between the squares, spreading over the surface but leaving a narrow border around the edges. Scatter over the Cashel Blue cheese.

Transfer the pastries to a large baking sheet and bake in a preheated oven, 220°C (425°F), Gas Mark 7, for 12–15 minutes until the pastry is puffed and the cheese is golden. Leave to cool slightly and serve warm.

PEA & LEEK OMELETTE

Serves 4
Preparation time 10 minutes
Cooking time 15–20 minutes

250 g (8 oz) baby new potatoes
75 g (3 oz) butter
1 tablespoon olive oil
500 g (1 lb) leeks, trimmed,
  cleaned and cut into 1 cm
  (½ inch) slices

200 g (7 oz) frozen or fresh peas
6 eggs
150 ml (5 fl oz) milk
2 tablespoons chopped chives
125 g (4 oz) soft garlic and chive
  cheese
salt and pepper

Cook the potatoes in boiling water for about 10 minutes or until cooked but
still firm.

Meanwhile, melt the butter with the oil in a large frying pan with a heatproof handle,
add the leeks, cover and cook, stirring frequently, for 8–10 minutes or until soft.
Stir in the peas.

Drain the potatoes, cut them into quarters and add to the frying pan. Continue
cooking for 2–3 minutes.

Whisk the eggs with the milk and chives, season well and pour into the frying pan.
Move around with a spatula so that the vegetables are well coated and the egg
begins to cook. Crumble the cheese on top and leave over a medium heat for
2–3 minutes until the egg becomes firm.

Place under a preheated hot grill for 3–4 minutes until the omelette is completely
set and the top is golden brown. Serve in thick slices.

PUMPKIN, LEEK & POTATO BAKE

Serves 4
Preparation time 30 minutes
Cooking time 2 hours

4 tablespoons hot horseradish
    sauce
1 tablespoon chopped thyme
300 ml (½ pint) double cream
1 large leek, trimmed, cleaned and
    finely shredded

100 g (3½ oz) walnuts, roughly
    chopped
500 g (1 lb) pumpkin
750 g (1½ lb) baking potatoes,
    thinly sliced
150 ml (¼ pint) vegetable stock
50 g (2 oz) breadcrumbs
40 g (1½ oz) butter, melted
2 tablespoons pumpkin seeds
salt

Mix the horseradish sauce in a large bowl with the thyme and half the cream.
Add the leek and all but 2 tablespoons of the walnuts and mix well.

Cut the pumpkin into chunks, discarding the skin and seeds. Thinly slice the chunks.

Scatter half the potatoes in a 2 litre (3½ pint) shallow, ovenproof dish, seasoning
lightly with salt, and cover with half the pumpkin chunks. Spoon the leek mixture
on top, spreading in an even layer. Arrange the remaining pumpkin slices on top
and then the remaining potato slices. Sprinkle with salt.

Mix the remaining cream with the stock and pour over the potatoes. Mix the
breadcrumbs with the butter and sprinkle over the top. Scatter with the pumpkin
seeds and remaining nuts. Cover with foil and bake in a preheated oven,
180°C (350°F), Gas Mark 4, for 1 hour. Remove the foil and bake for a further
45–60 minutes until golden and the vegetables feel tender when pierced with
a knife.

Serve with a crisp, green salad

FISH & SEAFOOD

ABUNDANT FISH SUPPLIES IN RIVERS AND LAKES AND IN THE SEA

around Ireland draw fishermen and tourists from all over the world to sample the harvest. Cooks around the country prepare modern and traditional dishes using the seasonal catch.

DEVILLED OYSTERS

Oysters are such a key part of its food heritage that the Emerald Isle has a dedicated season when food festivals around the country celebrate them.

Serves 4
Preparation time 25 minutes
Cooking time 15 minutes

12 oysters
1 teaspoon mustard seeds
75 g (3 oz) butter
2 shallots, finely chopped

½ celery stick, finely chopped
1 garlic clove, crushed
1 tablespoon white wine vinegar
1 teaspoon Tabasco sauce
1 tablespoon chopped chives
1 tablespoon chopped flat leaf
   parsley
plenty of sea salt and pepper

Hold an oyster, wrapped in a heavyweight cloth, with the rounded shell underneath. Push a strong knife, preferably an oyster knife, into the small gap at the hinged end. Twist the knife to sever the muscle and separate the shells.

Discard the top shell. Run the blade of the knife under the oyster to loosen it, holding the shell steady to prevent the juices from running out. Place the oyster in a grill pan, lined with a layer of salt to keep the shells from flopping over, and repeat with the remainder.

Dry-fry the mustard seeds in a frying pan until they start to pop. Add the butter, the shallots and celery and fry for 3 minutes. Add the garlic and a little salt and pepper and fry for a further 2 minutes. Stir in the vinegar, Tabasco sauce and two-thirds of each herb.

Spoon the mixture over the oysters and then cook under a preheated grill for 5–8 minutes, or until the oysters are just firm. Serve scattered with the remaining herbs.

GRILLED LEMON OYSTERS WITH SPINACH

Serves 4
Preparation time 10 minutes
Cooking time 20 minutes

1 tablespoon olive oil
150 g (5 oz) spinach
100 g (3½ oz) butter

2 egg yolks
lemon juice, to taste
1 teaspoon Worcestershire sauce
pinch of cayenne
12 live oysters, opened but in
 the shell
salt and pepper

Heat the oil in a large saucepan. Add the spinach and a splash of water and cook for 2 minutes until wilted. Drain, pressing out the liquid, and finely chop.

Melt the butter in a small saucepan until bubbling but not browned. Set a small heatproof bowl over a saucepan of simmering water, ensuring that the bottom of the bowl doesn't touch the water. Add the egg yolks and a good squeeze of lemon juice and whisk together. Whisking continuously, very slowly start to add the melted butter.

As the mixture starts to thicken, you can add the butter a little more quickly. When thickened, season and add more lemon juice to taste, the Worcestershire sauce and cayenne.

Discard the flat top shell of each oyster. Place a little spinach in each shell and sprinkle with more cayenne. Sit the oysters on a baking sheet and spoon over the sauce. Cook under a hot grill for 1 minute until the sauce has lightly browned.

MUSSELS WITH CIDER & GARLIC SAUCE

Serves 2
Preparation time 10 minutes
Cooking time 10 minutes

1 kg (2 lb) live mussels
15 g (½ oz) butter
1 garlic clove, chopped

100 ml (3½ fl oz) dry cider
2 tablespoons double cream
1 tablespoon chopped thyme
  leaves
salt and pepper
crusty bread, to serve

Scrub the mussels. Scrape off any barnacles and pull away any beards. Discard those that are damaged or open and do not close when tapped firmly.

Melt the butter in a large saucepan, add the garlic and cook gently for 1 minute. Tip in the mussels and add the cider. Bring to the boil, then cover and cook for 4–5 minutes, shaking the pan occasionally until the mussels have opened.

Using a slotted spoon, transfer the mussels to serving bowls, discarding any that remain closed. Reheat the pan juices, add the cream and thyme and season. Pour over the mussels and serve with crusty bread.

Serve plenty of bread to soak up the tasty juices

MUSSEL & POTATO HOTPOT

Serves 2
Preparation time 15 minutes
Cooking time 30 minutes

1 kg (2 lb) live mussels
25 g (1 oz) butter
1 onion, chopped
3 garlic cloves, crushed

150 ml (¼ pint) dry white
  wine
500 g (1 lb) baby potatoes,
  scrubbed
50 g (2 oz) curly parsley, roughly
  chopped
150 ml (¼ pint) single cream
salt and pepper

Scrub the mussels. Scrape off any barnacles and pull away any beards. Discard those that are damaged or open and do not close when tapped firmly.

Melt the butter in a large saucepan and gently fry the onion for 5 minutes until softened, adding the garlic for the last couple of minutes. Pour in the wine and bring to the boil. Tip the mussels into the pan, cover and cook, shaking the pan often, for 4–5 minutes until all the shells are open. Lift out with a slotted spoon into a bowl.

Add the potatoes to the cooking juices in the pan, re-cover and cook gently for 15 minutes or until the potatoes are cooked through, adding a little water if the pan runs dry. Meanwhile, remove about two-thirds of the mussels from their shells, discarding any closed shells.

Place the parsley and cream in a food processor and process until the parsley is finely chopped. Pour into the pan. Bring to the boil and boil briefly until the juices have thickened slightly. Return all the mussels to the pan and heat through gently for a couple of minutes. Season with pepper and a little salt and serve in bowls.

MINI SMOKED TROUT QUICHES

Serves 4
Preparation time 10 minutes
Cooking time 15–20 minutes

½ tablespoon rapeseed oil
400 g (13 oz) baby spinach leaves
6 large eggs
100 ml (3½ fl oz) milk

3 tablespoons Parmesan cheese, grated
2 tablespoons finely chopped chives
150 g (5 oz) hot-smoked trout fillets, flaked
4 cherry tomatoes, halved
salt and pepper

Line 8 holes of a muffin tin with 15 cm (6 inch) squares of greaseproof paper.

Heat the oil in a frying pan, add the spinach and cook briefly until wilted. Remove from the heat.

Beat together the eggs, milk and cheese in a jug and season to taste, then stir in the chives and trout.

Divide the spinach between the muffin cases, then pour in the egg mixture. Top each one with half a tomato. Bake in a preheated oven, 180°C (350°F), Gas Mark 4, for 12–15 minutes until just set.

Great for picnics or brunch

SMOKED MACKEREL & HORSERADISH PÂTÉ

Serves 4
Preparation time 10 minutes

500 g (1½ lb) smoked mackerel
  fillets
2 tablespoons natural yogurt
2 teaspoons creamed horseradish
juice of ½ lemon
pepper
oatcakes, toast or crudités,
  to serve

Skin and flake the mackerel into a
bowl. Add the remaining ingredients
and mix well.

Serve with oatcakes, toast or with
crudités.

Makes a simple but tasty starter

MACKEREL WITH BAKED BEETROOT

Serves 4
Preparation time 15 minutes
Cooking time 1 hour 5 minutes

4 small mackerel, filleted
1 tablespoon olive oil
salt and pepper

baked beetroot
2 large raw beetroot
2 garlic cloves, sliced

4 thyme sprigs
2 tablespoons olive oil, plus extra
for drizzling

horseradish cream
150 ml (¼ pint) crème fraîche
2 tablespoons mayonnaise
2 tablespoons finely chopped
chives
1–2 tablespoons creamed
horseradish

Wash the beetroot well. Wrap the beetroot in a foil parcel with the garlic, thyme, salt and pepper to taste and oil. Place in a preheated oven, 180°C (350°F), Gas Mark 4, for around 1 hour until the beetroot is cooked and a knife can easily be inserted into the centre. Once cool enough to handle, peel the beetroot. Cut into bite-sized pieces, drizzle with a little oil and season with salt and pepper. Set aside.

Mix together all the ingredients for the horseradish cream and season with salt and pepper.

Place the fish on a nonstick baking sheet, skin-side up. Brush the skin with the oil and season with salt and pepper. Cook under a preheated grill on this side until the skin is crispy, about 3 minutes, then carefully turn over and cook for a further 2 minutes on the other side.

Serve the mackerel with the baked beetroot and horseradish cream.

FISH PIE

Serves 4
Preparation time 15 minutes
Cooking time 25–30 minutes

750 g (1½ lb) floury potatoes,
   cut into chunks
2 eggs (optional)
400 ml (14 fl oz) full-fat milk
50 g (2 oz) plain flour
100 g (3½ oz) butter
2 tablespoons chopped parsley
25 g (1 oz) watercress, roughly
   chopped (optional)

390 g (12¾ oz) shop-bought
   fish pie mixture (available
   from the chilled section of
   supermarkets), or use bite-sized
   chunks of salmon, white fish
   fillet and smoked haddock
200 g (7 oz) raw peeled king
   prawns
3 tablespoons crème fraîche
75 g (3 oz) Cheddar cheese,
   grated
salt and pepper

Cook the potatoes in a pan of lightly salted boiling water for 10–12 minutes,
until tender.

Meanwhile, hard-boil the eggs, if using, in a pan of simmering water for about
8 minutes. Drain and hold under cold running water. Once cool enough to handle,
remove the shells and cut the eggs into wedges.

Place the milk, flour and half the butter in a saucepan and bring slowly to the
boil, stirring constantly with a balloon whisk, until thick and smooth. Simmer for
1–2 minutes, then season lightly and take off the heat.

Stir the parsley, watercress, if using, fish, prawns and egg into the sauce, then
transfer to an ovenproof dish.

Drain the potatoes and mash them with the crème fraîche and the remaining
butter. Season to taste, then spoon over the fish mixture and scatter with the
grated cheese. Place the pie in a preheated oven, 220°C (425°F), Gas Mark 7,
for 12–15 minutes, until golden and bubbling and the fish is cooked.

SALMON WITH HORSERADISH CRUST

Serves 4
Preparation time 10 minutes
Cooking time 12–15 minutes

4 salmon fillets, about 200 g (7 oz)
   each, skin on and pin-boned
4 tablespoons mild horseradish
   sauce

125 g (4 oz) fresh breadcrumbs
20 asparagus spears, trimmed
1 tablespoon olive oil
4–5 tablespoons crème fraîche
4 tablespoons lemon juice
1 tablespoon chopped parsley
salt and pepper

Place the salmon fillets in an ovenproof dish, skin-side down. Spread the top
of each fillet with 1 tablespoon of the horseradish sauce, then sprinkle with
the breadcrumbs. Place in a preheated oven, 180°C (350°F), Gas Mark 4, for
12–15 minutes until the fish is cooked and the breadcrumbs are golden brown.

Meanwhile, blanch the asparagus in salted boiling water for 2 minutes. Drain
and place in a very hot griddle pan with the oil to char slightly. Season with salt
and pepper.

Mix together the crème fraîche, lemon juice and parsley and season with salt
and pepper.

Serve the salmon with the chargrilled asparagus and lemon crème fraîche.

A light and delicately flavoured supper

SALMON FISHCAKES WITH DILL SAUCE

Fishcakes in Ireland were traditionally made with salmon because it was free for the catching. This modern variation on fishcakes adds a quick and easy dill sauce.

Serves 4
Preparation time 15 minutes
Cooking time 30 minutes

450 g (14½ oz) potatoes, peeled and cubed
3 tablespoons olive oil
500 g (1 lb) skinless salmon fillet
1 tablespoon chopped dill
finely grated rind of 1 lemon

plain flour, for dusting
1 egg, beaten
75 g (3 oz) dried breadcrumbs
salt and pepper
green salad, to serve

dill sauce
3 tablespoons mayonnaise
3 tablespoons natural yogurt
handful of dill, chopped
1 cornichon, sliced

Cook the potatoes in a saucepan of lightly salted boiling water for 12 minutes until soft. Drain well and roughly mash.

Meanwhile, rub 1 teaspoon of the oil over the salmon and season well. Cook under a preheated hot grill for 10 minutes until cooked through. Leave to cool a little, then break into large flakes. Mix together the ingredients for the sauce.

Mix together the potato, salmon, dill and lemon rind. Lightly wet your hands, then shape into 8 fishcakes. Dust each fishcake with a little flour, dip into the egg and finally dip into the breadcrumbs until well coated.

Heat the remaining oil in a large, nonstick frying pan. Cook the fishcakes for 3–4 minutes on each side until golden and crisp. Serve with a green salad and the dill sauce.

WHILE TRADITIONAL DISHES SUCH AS ROAST LEG OF LAMB are still the centrepiece of weekend family dinners, modern Irish cooking also uses the best the country's pastures have to offer – aged beef, mountain lamb, succulent pork – in new and enticing ways.

MEAT

LAMB CUTLETS WITH PEA & ROSEMARY MASH

Serves 4
Preparation time 10 minutes
Cooking time 15 minutes

750 g (1 lb 10 oz) potatoes, peeled and chopped

350 g (11½ oz) frozen or fresh peas
1 tablespoon chopped rosemary
8 lamb cutlets
30 g (1 oz) butter
salt and pepper

Cook the potatoes in a pan of boiling water for 12–15 minutes until tender, adding the peas 2 minutes before the end of the cooking time.

Meanwhile, sprinkle half the rosemary over the lamb cutlets then cook them under a preheated hot grill for 3–4 minutes on each side, or until cooked to your liking. Leave to rest.

Drain the potatoes and peas, then return to the pan and lightly mash with the remaining rosemary, butter and salt and pepper to taste. Serve the lamb cutlets accompanied by the pea and rosemary mash

A modern take on traditional mash

ROSEMARY-CRUSTED ROAST LAMB

Serves 4
Preparation time 10 minutes
Cooking time 30 minutes

750 g (1½ lb) small new potatoes, halved
300 g (10 oz) small chantenay carrots
3 tablespoons olive oil

3 tablespoons Dijon mustard
2 garlic cloves, crushed
2 racks of lamb, 7–8 bones each
1 tablespoon chopped rosemary
50 g (2 oz) dried breadcrumbs
2 teaspoons balsamic vinegar
2 tablespoons redcurrant jelly
75 ml (3 fl oz) chicken or lamb stock
salt and pepper

Toss the potatoes and carrots with 2 tablespoons of the oil and season well. Place in a large, shallow roasting tin and cook in a preheated oven, 220°C (425°F), Gas Mark 7, for 5 minutes.

Meanwhile, mix the remaining oil with the mustard and garlic and season to taste. Spread over the skin of the lamb, then scatter the rosemary and breadcrumbs on top and press lightly into place.

Arrange the lamb racks in the roasting tin and cook for 20 minutes until the vegetables are tender and the lamb is cooked to your liking, then remove the lamb and vegetables from the tin and keep warm.

Place the roasting tin over a gentle heat on the hob and add the balsamic vinegar, redcurrant jelly and stock. Allow to bubble for 2 minutes, then serve with the meat and vegetables.

STEAK & IRISH ALE STEW

Serves 5–6
Preparation time 20 minutes
Cooking time 1 hour 45 minutes

2 tablespoons plain flour
1 kg (2 lb) braising steak, cut
  into chunks
25 g (1 oz) butter
1 tablespoon oil
2 onions, chopped

2 celery sticks, sliced
several thyme sprigs
2 bay leaves
400 ml (14 fl oz) Irish ale
300 ml (½ pint) beef stock
2 tablespoons black treacle
500 g (1 lb) parsnips, peeled
  and cut into wedges
salt and pepper

Season the flour with salt and pepper and use to coat the beef. Melt the butter with the oil in a large, flameproof casserole and fry the beef in batches until deep brown. Drain with a slotted spoon while cooking the remainder.

Add the onions and celery and fry gently for 5 minutes. Return the beef to the pan and add the herbs, ale, stock and treacle. Bring just to the boil, then reduce the heat and cover with a lid. Bake in a preheated oven, 160°C (325°F), Gas Mark 3, for 1 hour.

Add the parsnips to the dish and return to the oven for a further 30 minutes or until the beef and parsnips are tender. Check the seasoning and serve.

Serve with creamy mashed potato for a hearty supper

BEEF, PICKLED ONION & GUINNESS STEW

Serves 4
Preparation time 10 minutes
Cooking time 2 hours 15 minutes

3 tablespoons plain flour
1 kg (2 lb) braising steak
2 tablespoons olive oil
500 g (1 lb) jar pickled onions,
    drained

2 carrots, thickly sliced
300 ml (½ pint) Guinness
600 ml (1 pint) beef stock
4 tablespoons tomato purée
1 tablespoon Worcestershire
    sauce
2 bay leaves
salt and pepper
chopped parsley, to garnish

Season the flour with salt and pepper on a plate. Cut the beef into large chunks and coat with the flour.

Heat the oil in a large flameproof casserole and fry the beef in batches until browned on all sides, lifting out with a slotted spoon on to a plate. Return all the beef to the casserole.

Stir the pickled onions and carrots into the casserole, then gradually blend in the Guinness and stock. Bring to the boil, stirring, then add the tomato purée, Worcestershire sauce, bay leaves and salt and pepper to taste.

Cover and cook in a preheated oven, 160°C (325°F), Gas Mark 3, for 2 hours, stirring halfway through, until the beef and vegetables are tender. Garnish with chopped parsley and serve immediately.

SAUSAGES WITH SPROUT COLCANNON

This winter warmer is a new take on Irish favourite, colcannon, using Brussels sprouts instead of the traditional kale or cabbage.

Serves 2
Preparation time 15 minutes
Cooking time 20 minutes

4 flavoured sausages, such as pork
   and apple
400 g (13 oz) floury potatoes, cut
   into chunks

50 g (2 oz) butter
200 g (7 oz) Brussels sprouts,
   sliced or shredded
¼ teaspoon freshly grated nutmeg
1 tablespoon chopped chives
1 tablespoon wholegrain mustard
2 tablespoons crème fraîche
salt and pepper

Arrange the sausages on a foil-lined grill rack and slide under a preheated, medium-hot grill for 15–18 minutes, or according to the packet instructions, until cooked through.

Meanwhile, cook the potatoes in a pan of salted boiling water for 12–15 minutes, until tender.

Meanwhile, melt half the butter in a frying pan and cook the sprouts with the nutmeg and a generous pinch of salt and pepper over a medium-low heat for 4–6 minutes, stirring occasionally, until softened.

Drain the potatoes, return to the pan and mash until smooth with the remaining butter. Stir in the chives, mustard, crème fraîche and sprouts and serve with the grilled sausages.

FARMHOUSE SAUSAGE & KALE STEW

Serves 4
Preparation time 10 minutes
Cooking time 40 minutes

1 tablespoon olive oil
150 g (5 oz) lean smoked bacon,
   chopped
3–4 herby pork sausages, about
   250 g (8 oz) in total, thickly sliced
1 onion, chopped
3 garlic cloves, chopped
1 leek, trimmed, cleaned and sliced
400 g (13 oz) can chopped
   tomatoes

2 tablespoons tomato purée
1 teaspoon dried oregano
pinch of sugar
300 ml (½ pint) golden ale or
   chicken stock
1 large potato, about 300 g (10 oz),
   peeled and roughly diced
400 g (13 oz) can borlotti beans,
   drained
200 g (7 oz) kale, shredded
salt and pepper
2 tablespoons chopped parsley,
   to garnish

Heat the oil in a large, heavy-based saucepan over a medium-high heat, add the
bacon and sausages and cook for 3–4 minutes or until browned. Add the onion,
garlic and leek, reduce the heat slightly and cook for 5–6 minutes until softened,
stirring occasionally.

Stir in the tomatoes, tomato purée, dried oregano, sugar and ale or stock and bring
to the boil. Stir in the potatoes and beans and season with salt and pepper. Reduce
the heat, cover and simmer gently for 20 minutes or until the potatoes are almost
tender. Stir in the kale, check the seasoning and cook for a further 8–10 minutes or
until the kale and potatoes are tender.

Ladle into bowls and sprinkle with the parsley. Serve immediately.

ROAST PORK LOIN WITH CREAMY CABBAGE & LEEKS

Serves 4
Preparation time 15 minutes
Cooking time 25–30 minutes

1 teaspoon ground cumin
1 teaspoon ground coriander
500 g (1 lb) pork loin, trimmed of fat
3 tablespoons olive oil

300 g (10 oz) sweet potatoes, peeled and chopped
250 g (8 oz) savoy cabbage, shredded
3 leeks, trimmed, cleaned and sliced
3 tablespoons soured cream
2 teaspoons wholegrain mustard

Mix together the spices in a bowl, then rub over the pork. Heat 1 tablespoon of the oil in an ovenproof frying pan, add the pork and cook until browned on all sides. Transfer to a preheated oven, 180°C (350°F), Gas Mark 4, and cook for 20–25 minutes or until cooked through. Leave to rest for 2 minutes.

Meanwhile, cook the sweet potatoes in a pan of boiling water for 12–15 minutes until tender, adding the cabbage and leeks 3–4 minutes before the end of the cooking time. Drain well.

Heat the remaining oil in a frying pan, add the vegetables and fry for 7–8 minutes until starting to turn golden. Stir in the cream and mustard.

Slice the pork and serve on top of the vegetables.

SPICED CABBAGE & BACON PAN-FRY

Serves 2
Preparation time 15 minutes
Cooking time 15 minutes

2 tablespoons olive oil
100 g (3½ oz) thick bacon rashers,
  cut into 1 cm (½ inch) strips
1 small onion, finely sliced
2 garlic cloves, chopped
pinch of ground allspice
pinch of ground cinnamon
¼ teaspoon grated nutmeg
½ small head savoy cabbage,
  thinly shredded
200 g (7 oz) cauliflower florets
salt and pepper
2 tablespoons chopped parsley,
  to garnish

Heat the oil in a large frying pan and cook the bacon for 2–3 minutes over a medium-high heat, until golden. Add the onion and garlic and cook for a further 3–4 minutes, until beginning to soften.

Stir in the spices until aromatic, then add the cabbage and cauliflower and stir-fry for 7–8 minutes, until slightly softened but still with some bite.

Season to taste, garnish with parsley, then heap into bowls to serve.

PORK CHOPS BAKED WITH POTATOES & BACON

Serves 4
Preparation time 10 minutes
Cooking time 45–50 minutes

750 g (1½ lb) potatoes, peeled
2 tablespoons extra virgin
  olive oil
4 large pork chops, about 250 g
  (8 oz) each

125 g (4 oz) piece of smoked
  bacon, rind removed, diced
1 large onion, sliced
2 garlic cloves, chopped
2 teaspoons dried oregano
grated rind and juice of 1 lemon
250 ml (8 fl oz) chicken stock
salt and pepper
a few thyme leaves, to garnish
  (optional)

Cut the potatoes into 2.5 cm (1 inch) cubes. Heat the oil in an ovenproof frying pan or flameproof casserole, add the pork chops and cook over a high heat for 1–2 minutes on each side until browned. Remove from the pan with a slotted spoon.

Reduce the heat to medium, add the bacon and onion and cook, stirring, for 3–4 minutes until golden. Add the potatoes, garlic, oregano and lemon rind and stir well. Pour in the stock and lemon juice and season lightly with salt and pepper.

Transfer to a preheated oven, 180°C (350°F), Gas Mark 4, and bake, uncovered, for 20 minutes. Arrange the chops on top and bake for a further 20 minutes until the potatoes and pork are cooked through. Garnish with thyme leaves, if liked, before serving.

A simple supper cooked in one dish

ONCE REGARDED AS A LUXURY FOR MOST IN IRELAND, CHICKEN
is widely used in contemporary Irish cuisine in dishes both rustic
and more sophisticated. Many cooks are also rediscovering
native specialities such as venison and pheasant.

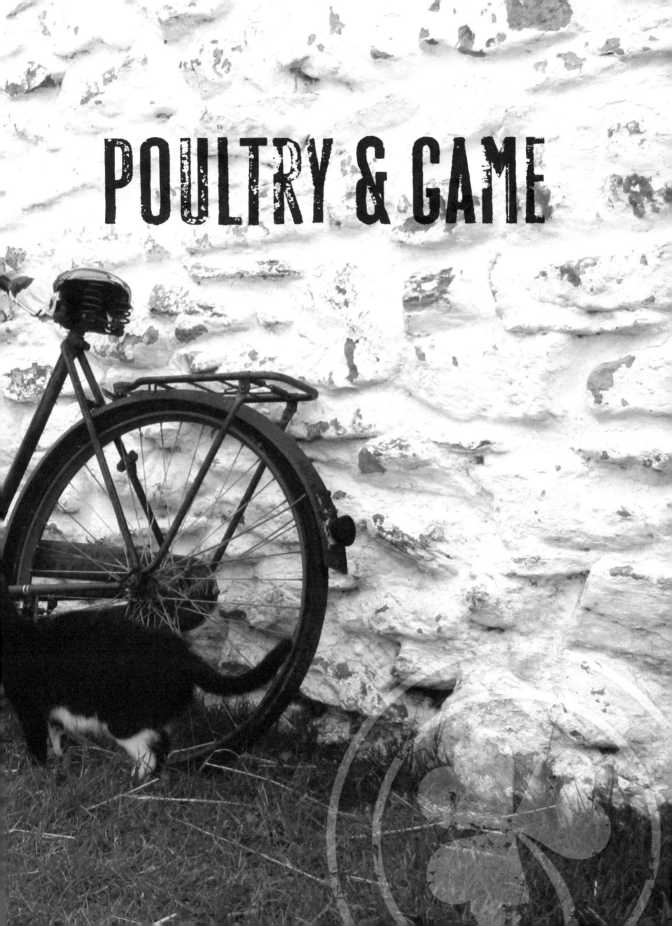

POULTRY & GAME

HERB & BACON CHICKEN ROAST

Serves 4
Preparation time 10 minutes
Cooking time 45 minutes

2 tablespoons extra virgin olive oil
2 tablespoons chopped thyme
2 garlic cloves, crushed
grated rind and juice of 1 lemon

4 chicken quarters, about
   375 g (12 oz) each
4 streaky bacon rashers, rind
   removed
1 tablespoon plain flour
150 ml (¼ pint) dry white wine
300 ml (½ pint) chicken stock
salt and pepper

Combine the oil, thyme, garlic, lemon rind and salt and pepper to taste in a bowl.
Score the chicken quarters several times with a sharp knife and rub all over with
the oil and herb mixture. Wrap each chicken quarter with bacon using cocktail sticks
to secure in place.

Transfer to a roasting tin and roast in a preheated oven, 200°C (400°F), Gas Mark 6,
 for 35–40 minutes until crisp and golden. Remove from the oven, transfer the
chicken pieces to a warm platter and wrap with foil.

Pour off all but 2 tablespoons fat from the roasting tin and place the tin over a
medium heat. Add the flour and cook, stirring constantly, for 30 seconds. Gradually
whisk in the wine and then the stock and simmer for 5 minutes until thickened.
Serve with the chicken.

Serve with crispy roast potatoes

TARRAGON CHICKEN WITH POTATOES

Serves 2
Preparation time 10 minutes
  + marinating time
Cooking time 1 hour

2 chicken breasts, each cut into
  about 8 slices
4 tablespoons lemon juice
1 garlic clove, crushed
handful of tarragon, chopped
25 g (1 oz) butter
125 g (4 oz) mixed mushrooms,
  sliced

200 ml (7 fl oz) double cream
salt and pepper
green beans, to serve

sliced potatoes
3 large unpeeled potatoes, thinly
  sliced
1 teaspoon finely chopped thyme
  leaves
1 tablespoon olive oil
150 ml (¼ pint) vegetable stock
5 g (¼ oz) butter

Layer the potato slices and thyme in a well-greased, ovenproof dish. Mix together the oil and stock and pour over the potatoes. Dot over the butter, cover with foil and bake in a preheated oven, 160°C (325°F), Gas Mark 3, for 1 hour, removing the foil halfway through cooking.

Meanwhile, put the chicken in a non-metallic dish. Mix together the lemon juice, garlic and tarragon, pour the mixture over the chicken and leave to marinate for 30 minutes.

Heat the butter in a frying pan and fry the mushrooms, then add the chicken and any juices and fry for a further 3 minutes. Add the cream to the pan and season with salt and pepper. Simmer gently for a couple of minutes until the chicken is just cooked. Serve with the sliced potatoes and steamed green beans.

CIDER & CHICKEN PIE

Serves 4
Preparation time 40 minutes
Cooking time 1 hour 20 minutes

8 chicken thighs
300 ml (½ pint) dry cider
300 ml (½ pint) chicken stock
2 small leeks, trimmed, cleaned
  and sliced

50 g (2 oz) butter
50 g (2 oz) plain flour
1 tablespoon chopped tarragon
2 tablespoons chopped parsley
500 g (1 lb) puff pastry, defrosted
  if frozen
flour, for dusting
beaten egg, to glaze
salt and pepper

Pack the chicken thighs into a saucepan, pour over the cider and stock, then season. Cover and simmer for 45 minutes.

Lift the chicken on to a plate, and simmer the leeks in the stock for 4–5 minutes. Strain the leeks, reserving the stock in a measuring jug. Make up the stock to 600 ml (1 pint) with water, if needed.

Wash and dry the pan, then melt the butter in it. Stir in the flour, then gradually whisk in the stock and bring to the boil, stirring until thickened. Mix in the herbs and season.

Dice the chicken, discarding the skin and bones. Put into a 1.2 litre (2 pint) pie dish with the leeks. Pour over the sauce.

Roll out the pastry on a floured surface until a little larger than the top of the pie dish. Cut 4 strips about 1 cm (½ inch) wide and stick along the rim with a little egg. Brush the top of the strip with egg, then press the pastry lid in place. Trim off the excess and crimp the edge. Cut leaves from the excess and place on top of the pie.

Glaze the pastry lid and bake in a preheated oven, 200°C (400°F), Gas Mark 6, for 30 minutes until golden.

SCONE-TOPPED CHICKEN & HAM PIE

Serves 4
Preparation time 15 minutes
Cooking time 20–25 minutes

2 tablespoons butter
2 leeks, sliced
300 g (10 oz) skinless, boneless
  chicken thighs, diced
150 g (5 oz) piece of ham, cut into
  small chunks
150 ml (¼ pint) hot chicken stock

100 ml (3½ fl oz) crème fraîche
150 g (5 oz) plain flour
1 tablespoon baking powder
2 tablespoons olive oil
150 ml (¼ pint) milk
2 tablespoons mixed herbs
  (such as parsley, thyme, chives),
  finely chopped
25 g (1 oz) Cheddar cheese,
  grated
salt and pepper

Melt the butter in a shallow, flameproof casserole dish. Add the leeks and cook for 3 minutes until softened. Add the chicken and cook for 2 minutes until lightly browned all over. Stir in the ham, stock and crème fraîche, then season to taste.

Mix the flour and baking powder in a bowl, then pour in the oil and milk. Mix gently, season well and stir in the herbs and cheese.

Arrange spoonfuls of the dough on top of the chicken mixture, leaving a little space between each spoonful. Place in a preheated oven, 220°C (425°F), Gas Mark 7, for 15–20 minutes until the topping is lightly browned and the chicken is cooked through.

A winter family favourite

ROAST DUCK WITH TURNIPS & REDCURRANTS

Serves 4
Preparation time 25 minutes
Cooking time 2 hours 15 minutes

4 large duck legs
¾ teaspoon ground cinnamon
1 kg (2 lb) potatoes, cut into 1.5 cm
  (¾ inch) dice
300 g (10 oz) turnips, cut into thin
  wedges

8 garlic cloves, peeled but left
  whole
1 tablespoon roughly chopped
  thyme
100 g (3½ oz) redcurrants
150 ml (¼ pint) chicken stock
3 tablespoons redcurrant jelly
4 tablespoons crème fraîche
salt and pepper

Halve the duck legs by cutting each through the joints. Mix the cinnamon with a little salt and pepper and rub over the duck legs. Arrange in a large roasting tin and roast in a preheated oven, 150°C (300°F), Gas Mark 2, for 1¼ hours.

Drain off most of the fat in the roasting tin, leaving just enough to coat the vegetables. Increase the oven temperature to 200°C (400°F), Gas Mark 6.

Add the potatoes, turnips, garlic and thyme to the roasting tin, turning them in the oil and seasoning lightly with salt and pepper. Return the roasting tin to the oven for 45 minutes until the vegetables are deep golden, turning frequently. Meanwhile, string the redcurrants by passing them between the tines of a fork.

Transfer the duck legs and vegetables to serving plates and keep warm. Drain off the excess fat in the roasting tin, leaving the meaty juices. Add the stock, redcurrant jelly and crème fraîche and bring to the boil on the hob. Cook until slightly reduced and thickened. Stir in the redcurrants, season to taste with salt and pepper and heat for 1 minute. Spoon over the duck to serve.

GAME PIE

Serves 4
Preparation time 45 minutes
Cooking time 2 hours

25 g (1 oz) butter
1 tablespoon olive oil
1 oven-ready pheasant, halved
1 oven-ready pigeon, halved
2 rabbit or chicken leg joints
1 large onion, roughly chopped
100 g (3½ oz) smoked streaky
    bacon, diced

2 tablespoons plain flour, plus
    extra for dusting
200 ml (7 fl oz) red wine
400 ml (13 fl oz) chicken stock
2 tablespoons redcurrant jelly
1 teaspoon juniper or allspice
    berries, roughly crushed
1 bouquet garni
375 g (12 oz) puff pastry, defrosted
    if frozen
beaten egg, to glaze
salt and pepper

Heat the butter and oil in a large frying pan, then fry the game, in batches, until browned. Lift out and put into a large casserole dish. Add the onion and bacon to the frying pan and fry for 5 minutes, stirring until golden. Mix in the flour, then stir in the wine, stock and redcurrant jelly. Add the berries, bouquet garni and seasoning, then bring to the boil. Tip the sauce over the game, cover and cook in a preheated oven, 160°C (325°F), Gas Mark 3, for 1¼ hours. Leave to cool.

Lift out the game and take the meat off the bone. Return the meat to the sauce, discard the bouquet garni, then spoon into a 1.2 litre (2 pint) pie dish.

Roll out the pastry on a lightly floured surface until a little larger than the top of the pie dish. Cut 1 cm (½ inch) wide strips from the edges and stick on to the dish rim with beaten egg. Brush the pastry strips with egg and lay the sheet of pastry on top. Press down, trim off the excess then flute the edges. Cut leaves from the rerolled trimmings and decorate.

Brush the pie with beaten egg, then cook in a preheated oven, 200°C (400°F), Gas Mark 6, for 30–35 minutes until golden and piping hot inside.

POACHER'S PIE

Serves 4
Preparation time 30 minutes
Cooking time 2 hours 10 minutes

15 g (½ oz) dried porcini
  mushrooms
150 ml (¼ pint) boiling water
75 g (3 oz) butter
1 tablespoon olive oil
700 g (1 lb 7 oz) venison, diced
1 onion, chopped

2 tablespoons plain flour
200 ml (7 fl oz) red wine
300 ml (½ pint) lamb stock
1 tablespoon tomato purée
2 tablespoons redcurrant jelly
750 g (1½ lb) potatoes
2 tablespoons milk
2–3 teaspoons hot creamed
  horseradish sauce
3 tablespoons chopped chives
salt and pepper

Soak the dried porcini mushrooms in the measurement boiling water in a small bowl for 15 minutes.

Meanwhile, heat one-third of the butter and the oil in a flameproof casserole and add the venison, a few pieces at a time. Add the onion and fry over a high heat for 5 minutes, stirring until browned.

Stir in the flour then mix in the wine, stock, mushrooms and soaking liquid, tomato purée and redcurrant jelly. Season then bring to the boil and cover the dish. Bake in a preheated oven, 160°C (325°F), Gas Mark 3, for 1 hour 15 minutes.

To make the topping, cook the potatoes in boiling water for 15 minutes until tender. Drain and mash with half the remaining butter and the milk. Stir in the horseradish, to taste, the chives and a little seasoning. Spoon the venison mixture into a 1.5 litre (2½ pint) pie dish. Spoon the potato over the top and dot with the remaining butter.

Stand the dish on a baking sheet then cook in a preheated oven, 190°C (375°F), Gas Mark 5, for 45–50 minutes until golden brown and piping hot.

VENISON, GUINNESS & CHESTNUT STEW

Serves 6
Preparation time 25 minutes
Cooking time 2 hours 15 minutes

3 tablespoons plain flour
1.25 kg (2½ lb) venison, diced
50 g (2 oz) butter
200 g (7 oz) pancetta or streaky
  bacon, chopped
1 small leek, trimmed, cleaned
  and chopped

3 carrots, diced
2 parsnips, diced
4 garlic cloves, crushed
2 teaspoons chopped rosemary
500 ml (17 fl oz) Guinness
300 ml (½ pint) beef stock
200 g (7 oz) pack cooked peeled
  chestnuts
500 g (1 lb) new potatoes, scrubbed
  and cut into small chunks
salt and pepper

Season the flour with salt and pepper on a plate. Coat the venison with the flour.

Melt the butter in a flameproof casserole and fry the venison in batches until browned, lifting out with a slotted spoon on to a plate. Add the pancetta or bacon, leek, carrots and parsnips to the casserole and fry gently for 6–8 minutes until lightly browned. Add the garlic, rosemary and any flour left over from coating, and cook, stirring, for 1 minute.

Blend in the Guinness and stock and bring to a simmer, stirring. Return the venison to the casserole, then reduce the heat, cover and cook very gently for 1½ hours or until the meat is tender. Add the chestnuts and potatoes and cook for a further 20 minutes or until the potatoes are cooked through. Season to taste with salt and pepper.

Serve with steamed kale or cabbage

NO IRISH MEAL IS COMPLETE WITHOUT A SWEET TREAT TO END IT.

For generations, cooks have made the most of fruit, including apples, rhubarb and gooseberries. These innovative recipes follow that tradition and some include a splash of Irish cheer in the form of whiskey too!

PUDDINGS

IRISH COFFEE GATEAU

Serves 8
Preparation time 30 minutes
  + cooling and chilling time
Cooking time 10 minutes

2 tablespoons instant coffee
  granules
100 ml (3½ fl oz) hot water
50 g (2 oz) caster sugar
3 tablespoons Irish whiskey

300 g (10 oz) plain dark chocolate,
  broken into pieces
300 ml (½ pint) double cream
200 g (7 oz) Greek yogurt
200 g (7 oz) savoiardi biscuits or
  sponge fingers

to decorate
plain dark or milk chocolate curls
cocoa powder, for dusting

Dissolve the coffee granules in a pan in the measurement hot water. Add the sugar and heat gently until the sugar dissolves. Bring to the boil and boil rapidly for 1 minute. Remove from the heat and leave to cool. Stir in the whiskey.

Melt the chocolate with half the cream in a bowl over a pan of simmering water. Remove from the heat and stir in the yogurt and remaining cream. Leave to thicken slightly.

Spread a thin layer of the chocolate mixture on to a flat plate, to make a 23 x 10 cm (9 x 4 inch) rectangle. Dip one-third of the biscuits or sponge fingers in the coffee syrup so they are softened but not soggy.

Arrange the dipped biscuits or fingers side by side on the chocolate, then spread over more chocolate mixture. Dip half the remaining biscuits or fingers in the syrup and arrange them as before over the chocolate. Spread more chocolate mixture on top, then cover with the remaining syrup-dipped biscuits or fingers.

Spread the remaining chocolate mixture over the top and sides of the cake to cover it completely, smoothing with the knife. Chill for 3–4 hours until set. Decorate with chocolate curls and dust with cocoa powder.

AUTUMN BERRY CRUMBLE

Serves 4
Preparation time 10 minutes
Cooking time 30–35 minutes

300 g (10 oz) cranberries
150 g (5 oz) blackberries
150 g (5 oz) blueberries
4 tablespoons water
75 g (3 oz) caster sugar

crumble topping
75 g (3 oz) fresh breadcrumbs
75 g (3 oz) ground almonds
75 g (3 oz) butter, diced
50 g (2 oz) caster sugar
25 g (1 oz) flaked almonds

Put the fruits into a saucepan with the measurement water, cover and cook over a gentle heat for 10 minutes or until just tender. Stir in the sugar then tip into a shallow ovenproof dish, leaving room for the crumble.

To make the crumble, put the breadcrumbs, ground almonds, butter and sugar into a bowl and rub the butter in with your fingertips until the mixture resembles fine crumbs.

Sprinkle the crumble over the top of the fruit. Sprinkle with the flaked almonds, then bake in a preheated oven, 190°C (375°F), Gas Mark 5, for 20–25 minutes until crisp and golden. Cover with foil after 15 minutes if it is getting too brown. Spoon into bowls and serve with just-melting scoops of vanilla ice cream or hot vanilla custard.

Serve with custard for a comforting dessert

APPLE & SULTANA POTS

Serves 4
Preparation time 15 minutes
Cooking time 15–20 minutes

2 lapsang souchong tea bags
1 tablespoon clear honey
3 tablespoons sultanas
3 dessert or cooking apples,
  peeled, cored and diced

½ teaspoon mixed spice
25 g (1 oz) dark brown sugar
25 g (1 oz) unsalted butter
150 g (5 oz) double cream,
  whipped to soft peaks
caster sugar, as required
ginger snaps, to serve

Make a strong infusion of tea using the tea bags in 100 ml (3½ fl oz) boiling water. Stir in the honey and sultanas and set aside to infuse.

Put the apples in a saucepan with the mixed spice, brown sugar and butter. Remove the teabags from the infusion and pour the liquid over the apples.

Cover and cook over a medium-low heat, stirring frequently, for 15–20 minutes until the apples start to collapse. Crush to a chunky purée.

Stir the double cream into the apple purée until well combined, then spoon the mixture into 4 individual ovenproof dishes.

Sprinkle the surface generously with caster sugar, then place the dishes under a hot grill until the sugar begins to caramelize. Serve warm or cold with ginger snaps.

Serve the pots warm or cold

INDIVIDUAL BLACKBERRY & APPLE CRUMBLES

Serves 4
Preparation time 10 minutes
Cooking time 25 minutes

4 dessert apples, peeled, cored
  and thinly sliced
125 g (4 oz) blackberries

2 teaspoons caster sugar
100 g (3½ oz) rolled oats
50 g (2 oz) unsalted butter,
  diced
40 g (1¾ oz) dark muscovado
  sugar
25 g (1 oz) flaked almonds

Divide the apple slices and blackberries between 4 small ovenproof dishes or ramekins and sprinkle with the caster sugar.

In a food processor, blitz the oats, butter, sugar and almonds. Spoon the oat mixture over the fruit and bake in a preheated oven, 190°C (375°F), Gas Mark 5, for 22–25 minutes until golden.

Serve with crème fraîche or ice cream

OLD BUSHMILLS DISTILLERY CO LIMITED
SINGLE MALT
1608
OLD BUSHMILLS DISTILLERY CO LIMITED
SINGLE MALT
1608
OLD BUSHMILLS DISTILLERY CO LIMITED
SINGLE MALT
1608
OLD BUSHMILLS DISTILLERY CO LIMITED
SINGLE MALT
1608

IRISH WHISKEY SYLLABUB

Liberally laced with Irish whiskey, which the Irish have been producing since the Middle Ages, this syllabub is equally delicious served immediately as a thick, creamy concoction or chilled for several hours, when it will separate into a two-layered version with thick cream on top and a clear liquid at the bottom.

Serves 4–6
Preparation time 15 minutes
  + standing and chilling time

rind and juice of 1 large lemon
6 tablespoons clear honey

8 tablespoons Irish whiskey
300 ml (½ pint) double
  cream
grated nutmeg, to decorate
shortbread fingers, to serve
  (optional)

Put the lemon rind and juice, honey and whiskey into a large bowl, cover and leave to stand for at least 2 hours or overnight, to develop the flavours.

Gradually whisk in the cream until the mixture begins to thicken then spoon into wine glasses, grate over a little nutmeg and serve immediately with shortbread fingers, if liked, or refrigerate until required.

Serve with crisp shortbread fingers

GOOSEBERRY & ELDERFLOWER PIES

Makes 4
Preparation time 30 minutes
  + chilling time
Cooking time 20–25 minutes

lemon-flavoured pâte sucrée
175 g (6 oz) plain flour
40 g (1½ oz) icing sugar
grated rind of 1 lemon
100 g (3½ oz) butter, diced
2 egg yolks

filling
125 g (4 oz) caster sugar, plus
  extra for sprinkling
2 teaspoons cornflour
400 g (13 oz) gooseberries,
  topped and tailed
1 tablespoon elderflower cordial,
  undiluted
milk or beaten egg, to glaze

To make pâte sucrée, place the flour, icing sugar, grated lemon rind and butter in a food processor or mixing bowl and mix until you have fine crumbs. Add the egg yolks and mix together until you have a soft ball. Wrap in clingfilm and chill for 15 minutes before using.

Mix the sugar, cornflour and gooseberries together in a bowl. Cut the pastry into 4 pieces, then roll each piece out to a rough-shaped 18 cm (7 inch) circle. Drape each piece into a buttered individual Yorkshire pudding tin, 10 cm (4 inches) in diameter and 2.5 cm (1 inch) deep, leaving the excess pastry overhanging the edges of the tins.

Spoon in the gooseberry mixture and mound up in the centre, then drizzle over the elderflower cordial. Fold the overhanging pastry up and over the filling, pleating where needed and leaving the centres of the pies open.

Brush the pastry with milk or beaten egg, sprinkle with a little sugar and bake in a preheated oven, 190°C (375°F), Gas Mark 5, for 20–25 minutes until golden. Leave to stand for 15 minutes, then loosen the edges and lift the pies out of the tins. Serve with cream.

RHUBARB FOOL

Serves 4
Preparation time 10 minutes
Cooking time 10 minutes

450 g (14½ oz) rhubarb, chopped
  into bite-sized pieces

2 tablespoons caster sugar
4 tablespoons white wine
300 ml (½ pint) double cream
finely grated rind of 1 lemon
1 egg white
chopped pistachios nuts, to serve

Place the rhubarb and sugar into a saucepan over a low heat, pour in the wine and simmer over a low heat until cooked. Pour into a bowl and leave to cool.

Whisk the cream until thick and stir into the rhubarb with the grated lemon rind.

Whisk the egg white until stiff, then gently fold into the rhubarb mixture.

Divide between 4 bowls and top with the chopped pistachios. Chill until required.

BAKED APPLES WITH SPICED FRUIT

Serves 4
Preparation time 10 minutes
Cooking time 25 minutes

4 cooking apples, cored and scored
   around the middle
75 g (3 oz) dried cranberries
4 pieces of preserved stem ginger,
   diced
finely grated rind of 2 oranges
½ teaspoon mixed spice
4 tablespoons clear honey
crème fraîche, to serve

Place the apples in an ovenproof dish. Mix
together the cranberries, ginger, orange
rind, mixed spice and honey and spoon
the mixture into the cavity of each apple.

Pour 2 tablespoons water into the dish. Bake in a preheated oven, 190°C (375°F),
Gas Mark 5, for 22–25 minutes until the apples are puffy and cooked through.
Serve with crème fraîche.

Try this with dates instead of cranberries

WARM SUMMER FRUIT TRIFLES

Makes 6
Preparation time 20 minutes
Cooking time 20 minutes

8 sponge fingers or 100 g
   (3½ oz) plain sponge or
   jam-filled swiss roll
3 tablespoons orange juice

375 g (12 oz) frozen mixed summer
   fruits, just defrosted
425 g (14 oz) ready-made custard

meringue topping
3 egg whites
75 g (3 oz) granulated sugar

Crumble the sponge fingers or cake into the bottom of 6 individual ovenproof dishes. Drizzle the orange juice over the tops, then add the mixed fruits. Dollop the custard over the tops.

Whisk the egg whites in a clean, dry bowl until stiff peaks form, then gradually whisk in the sugar, a spoonful at a time, until all the sugar has been added. Keep whisking for another 1–2 minutes until the mixture is thick and glossy.

Spoon the meringue mixture over the top of the custard in large swirls. Place the dishes on a baking sheet. Cook in a preheated oven, 160°C (325°F), Gas Mark 3, for 20 minutes until the meringue is golden brown on top. Serve warm.

WHIPPED IRISH CREAM HOT CHOCOLATE

Serves 4
Preparation time 10 minutes
Cooking time 5 minutes

200 g (7 oz) coarsely grated
dark chocolate, plus extra for
sprinkling

900 ml (1½ pints) milk
150 ml (¼ pint) double cream
1 tablespoon icing sugar
75 ml (3 fl oz) Irish cream liqueur
1–2 tablespoons caster sugar,
according to taste

Place the chocolate in a large heatproof jug. Heat the milk in a pan until it is almost simmering.

Meanwhile, whip the double cream with the icing sugar until it forms soft peaks, then fold in 1 tablespoon of the cream liqueur.

Pour about a quarter of the hot milk into the jug, stirring until the chocolate has melted. Add the remaining milk in a steady stream, stirring constantly. Add the remaining Irish cream and sweeten to taste with the caster sugar.

Pour the hot chocolate mixture into mugs and top with the desired quantity of whipped cream. Sprinkle with a little extra grated chocolate to decorate, and serve immediately.

A little cup of sheer luxury...

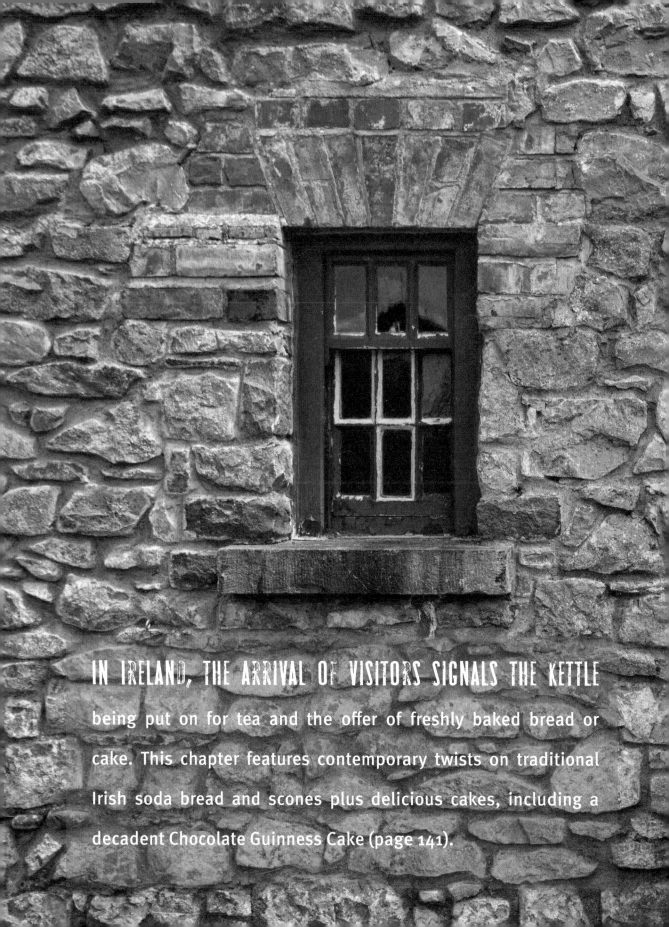

IN IRELAND, THE ARRIVAL OF VISITORS SIGNALS THE KETTLE being put on for tea and the offer of freshly baked bread or cake. This chapter features contemporary twists on traditional Irish soda bread and scones plus delicious cakes, including a decadent Chocolate Guinness Cake (page 141).

BREAD & CAKES

BOXTY

Meaning 'poorhouse bread', boxty are traditional potato pancakes found in the northern counties of Cavan, Donegal, Leitrim and Monaghan. They are also sometimes called stamp. They can be served with jam for breakfast, with bacon and eggs for a substantial brunch, or spread with butter and sprinkled with sugar as a sweet snack.

Makes about 10
Preparation time 20 minutes
Cooking time 20 minutes

500 g (1 lb) potatoes, peeled
2 tablespoons plain flour
1 teaspoon baking powder
150 ml (¼ pint) milk
vegetable oil, for frying
salt and pepper
jam, to serve

Serve with a dollop of your favourite jam

Coarsely grate the potatoes into a large bowl. Sieve in the flour and baking powder. Season with salt and pepper, add the milk and mix well.

Light oil a frying pan or griddle, heat over a medium heat and drop in tablespoons of the mixture. Cook for about 5 minutes on each side until golden brown. Keep warm and repeat with the remaining mixture.

Serve with a spoonful of jam.

SAFFRON & POTATO BUNS

Makes 12
Preparation time 20 minutes
  + cooling time
Cooking time 25 minutes

300 g (10 oz) potatoes, diced
½ teaspoon crumbled saffron
  strands
1 tablespoon boiling water
200 ml (7 fl oz) milk
4 tablespoons olive oil

1 egg, beaten
275 g (9 oz) plain flour
1 tablespoon baking powder
2 teaspoons chopped thyme,
  plus extra sprigs for sprinkling
1 teaspoon sea salt, plus extra
  for sprinkling
egg yolk lightly whisked with
  1 teaspoon water, for glazing
butter, to serve

Line a 12-section bun tray with paper cake cases. Cook the potatoes in a saucepan of salted boiling water for 8 minutes or until just tender. Drain and leave to cool.

Mix the saffron with the measurement boiling water in a jug and leave to stand for 5 minutes. Whisk together the saffron and water, milk, oil and egg with a fork in a bowl.

Mix together the flour, baking powder, chopped thyme and salt in a separate bowl, then stir in the potato.

Add the saffron mixture and mix with a large metal spoon until evenly combined.

Divide the mixture between the paper cases. Brush the tops lightly with the egg yolk mixture. Sprinkle with a little extra salt and scatter with thyme sprigs. Bake in a preheated oven, 220°C (425°F), Gas Mark 7, for 15 minutes or until risen and pale golden. Transfer to a wire rack. Serve warm or cold, split and buttered.

BACON, THYME & POTATO MUFFINS

Makes 12
Preparation time 20 minutes
  + cooling time
Cooking time 15–20 minutes

400 g (13 oz) waxy potatoes,
  peeled and diced
100 g (3½ oz) smoked streaky
  bacon, finely chopped

275 g (9 oz) self-raising flour
2 teaspoons baking powder
1 tablespoon chopped thyme,
  plus extra sprigs for scattering
175 ml (6 fl oz) milk
5 tablespoons olive oil
1 egg, beaten
salt and pepper

Cook the potatoes in a saucepan of salted boiling water for 5–6 minutes until softened. Drain and leave to cool.

Heat a dry frying pan and fry the bacon until golden and crisp. Leave to cool.

Mix together the flour, baking powder, chopped thyme and a little salt and pepper in a bowl. Stir in the potatoes and bacon. Beat together the milk, oil and egg in a jug. Add to the dry ingredients and stir together using a large metal spoon until just combined.

Divide the mixture evenly between paper muffin cases arranged in a 12-hole muffin tray. Sprinkle with a little salt and scatter with thyme. Bake in a preheated oven, 220°C (425°F), Gas Mark 7, for 15–20 minutes until risen and golden. Transfer to a wire rack to cool. Serve warm or cold, scattered with extra thyme sprigs.

A tempting teatime treat...

WHITE SODA BREAD

Popular throughout Ireland in various forms, all soda breads are best eaten on the day they are baked or toasted the following day. You can also find recipes for contemporary twists on this classic bread on pages 128–131.

Makes 1 loaf
Preparation time 10 minutes
Cooking time 1 hour

500 g (1 lb) soda bread flour, plus
  extra for dusting

1 teaspoon bicarbonate of soda
1 teaspoon salt
25 g (1 oz) caster sugar
400–475 ml (14–16 fl oz)
  buttermilk
24 g (1 oz) butter

Sift the flour, bicarbonate of soda and salt into a large mixing bowl. Add the sugar. Make a well in centre and pour in 400 ml (14 fl oz) of the buttermilk. Mix lightly with a broad-bladed knife or wooden spoon to form a spongy dough, adding more buttermilk if necessary. Mix quickly and lightly and don't overwork the dough.

Grease a 19 x 11 cm (7½ x 4½ inch) loaf tin with the butter and turn the porridge-like dough into the tin, spreading it into the corners but leaving the surface rough. Sprinkle with a little extra flour, place the tin on a baking sheet and bake in a preheated oven, 200°C (400°F), Gas Mark 6, for 30 minutes. Reduce the heat to 150°C (300°F), Gas Mark 2 and cook for a further 30 minutes, until the bread is well risen, pale beige and crusty on top.

Remove from the oven, cover with a clean tea towel and leave for 5 minutes, then turn the bread out of the tin, wrap in the cloth and leave to cool.

Note: If you can't find soda bread flour, use the same quantity of plain flour with 1 heaped teaspoon each of bicarbonate of soda and cream of tartar.

APRICOT & CHEESE SODA BREAD

Makes 1 loaf
Preparation time 10 minutes
  + cooling time
Cooking time 35–40 minutes

2 teaspoons sunflower oil
6 spring onions, thinly sliced
250 g (8 oz) plain flour
250 g (8 oz) plain wholemeal
  flour
2 teaspoons bicarbonate
  of soda
1 teaspoon salt
125 g (4 oz) Wensleydale cheese
  with apricots, crumbled
400 ml (14 fl oz) buttermilk, plus
  2 tablespoons for brushing

Heat the oil in a small frying pan, add the spring onions and cook gently for
2 minutes until softened. Leave to cool slightly.

Sift the flours, bicarbonate of soda and salt into a large bowl. Stir in the cheese
and spring onions. Make a well in the centre, add the buttermilk to the well and
gradually stir into the flour. Bring the mixture together with your hands to form a
soft, slightly sticky dough.

Tip the dough out on to a lightly floured surface and lightly knead for 1 minute,
then shape into a ball. Place on a lightly floured nonstick baking sheet and flatten
slightly. Make a deep cross in the top with a serrated knife. Brush the top with the
remaining buttermilk.

Bake in a preheated oven, 200°C (400°F), Gas Mark 6, for 30–35 minutes until the
loaf sounds hollow when tapped on the base. Leave to cool on a wire rack. It is best
served warm.

RED ONION & HERB SODA BREAD

Makes 1 loaf
Preparation time 15 minutes
  + standing time
Cooking time 30 minutes

325 ml (11 fl oz) milk, plus extra
  if required
1 tablespoon lemon juice
1 small red onion, finely chopped
1 egg, beaten
250 g (8 oz) plain wholemeal flour
250 g (8 oz) plain white flour,
  plus extra for dusting
2 teaspoons salt
1 teaspoon bicarbonate of soda
25 g (1 oz) mixed herbs, such as
  parsley, chervil, dill and chives,
  chopped
40 g (1½ oz) butter, diced

Mix together the milk and lemon juice in a jug and leave to stand for 5 minutes.
Stir in the onion and egg.

Put the flours, salt and bicarbonate of soda in a separate bowl and stir in the
herbs. Add the butter and rub in with the fingertips until the mixture resembles fine
breadcrumbs. Pour the milk mixture into the bowl and mix to a dough, adding a
little more milk if the dough feels dry.

Shape the dough into a ball on a lightly floured surface, then place on a greased
baking sheet and flatten slightly. Dust generously with extra flour. Using a sharp
knife, cut a 2.5 cm (1 inch) deep cross through the top of the dough.

Bake in a preheated oven, 200°C (400°F), Gas Mark 6, for about 30 minutes until
risen and deep golden. The base of the bread should sound hollow when tapped.
Transfer to a wire rack to cool.

MINI HERBED SODA BREADS

Makes 8
Preparation time 10 minutes
Cooking time 25–30 minutes

250 g (8 oz) wholemeal flour, plus
   extra for dusting
250 g (8 oz) plain flour
1 teaspoon bicarbonate of soda
1 teaspoon salt

50 g (2 oz) butter, chilled and
   diced, plus extra for greasing
1 spring onion, finely chopped
1 tablespoon chopped parsley
1 tablespoon chopped thyme
1 tablespoon chopped rosemary
275 ml (9 fl oz) buttermilk, or
   ordinary milk soured with
   1 tablespoon lemon juice

Sift the flours, bicarbonate of soda and salt into a bowl. Add the butter and rub in with your fingertips until the mixture resembles fine breadcrumbs. Add the spring onion and the herbs and mix well to combine. Make a well in the centre and add the buttermilk or soured milk. Mix with a round-bladed knife to make a soft dough. Turn out on to a lightly floured work surface and knead lightly into a ball. Divide the dough between 8 greased dariole moulds.

Place the dariole moulds on a baking sheet, flatten the dough slightly and dust with flour.

Bake in a preheated oven, 220°C (425°F), Gas Mark 7, for about 25–30 minutes until risen, golden and hollow sounding when tapped underneath. Transfer to a wire rack to cool. For a softer crust, wrap the hot breads in a clean tea towel to cool. Eat on the day they are made.

Delicious with some tangy Irish Cheddar

CHEESE & APPLE SCONES

Makes about 10
Preparation time 10 minutes
Cooking time 15–18 minutes

125 g (4 oz) self-raising flour, plus
  extra for dusting
100 g (3½ oz) wholemeal
  self-raising flour

40 g (1¾ oz) chilled butter, diced,
  plus extra to serve
1 teaspoon cumin seeds
75 g (3 oz) Cheddar cheese, grated
1 dessert apple, peeled, cored
  and diced
150 ml (¼ pint) milk
chutney, to serve

Sift the flours into a large bowl, add the butter and rub in with the fingertips until the mixture resembles fine breadcrumbs. Stir in the cumin seeds, two-thirds of the cheese and the apple, then add the milk and mix with a palette knife to a soft dough.

Turn the dough out on to a floured surface and press out to 1.5 cm (¾ inch) thick. Cut out about 10 rounds using a 5 cm (2 inch) plain biscuit cutter or glass, using the trimmings as necessary.

Place the scones on a baking sheet and sprinkle with the remaining cheese. Bake in a preheated oven, 220°C (425°F), Gas Mark 7, for 15–18 minutes until risen and golden. Transfer to a wire rack to cool or serve warm, spread with butter and chutney.

Use a tasty fruit chutney

WHOLEWHEAT TREACLE SCONES

Makes 14
Preparation time 15 minutes
Cooking time 6–8 minutes

400 g (13 oz) malted bread flour,
 plus extra for dusting and
 sprinkling (optional)
50 g (2 oz) butter, diced
50 g (2 oz) light muscovado sugar
3 teaspoons baking powder

1 teaspoon bicarbonate of soda
8 tablespoons low-fat natural
 yogurt
2 tablespoons black treacle
1 egg, beaten

to serve
whipped cream or crème frâiche
strawberry jam

Put the flour in a mixing bowl or a food processor. Add the butter and rub in with your fingertips or process until the mixture resembles fine breadcrumbs. Stir in the sugar and baking powder.

Stir the bicarbonate of soda into the yogurt then add to the flour mixture with the black treacle. Gradually mix in enough of the beaten egg to form a soft but not sticky dough. Knead lightly then roll out on a lightly floured surface until 2 cm (¾ inch) thick.

Working quickly, cut out 5.5 cm (2¼ inch) circles using a plain biscuit cutter. Transfer to a greased baking sheet. Reknead the trimmings and continue rolling and stamping out until all the mixture has been used. Add to the baking sheet and sprinkle the tops with a little extra flour or leave plain if preferred.

Bake in a preheated oven, 220°C (425°F), Gas Mark 7, for 6–8 minutes until well risen and browned. Serve warm or cold, split and topped with cream or crème frâiche and jam. They are best eaten on the day they are made.

POPPY SEED & APPLE TEABREAD

Serves 10
Preparation time 20 minutes
  + cooling time
Cooking time about 1 hour
  15 minutes

100 g (3½ oz) dried apples,
  roughly chopped
100 ml (3½ fl oz) water
175 g (6 oz) slightly salted butter,
  softened

finely grated rind of 2 lemons
3 tablespoons lemon juice
175 g (6 oz) caster sugar
3 eggs
250 g (8 oz) self-raising flour
50 g (2 oz) poppy seeds

lemon icing
75 g (3 oz) icing sugar, sifted
1 tablespoon lemon juice

Put the apples and measurement water in a small saucepan and heat for 5 minutes until the apples have absorbed the water. Leave to cool.

Beat together the remaining cake ingredients in a bowl until pale and creamy. Stir in the cooled apples.

Spoon the mixture into a greased and lined 1 kg (2 lb) or 1.3 litre (2¼ pint) loaf tin and level the surface. Bake in a preheated oven, 160°C (325°F), Gas Mark 3, for 1–1¼ hours or until firm to the touch and a skewer inserted into the centre comes out clean. Loosen the cake at the ends and transfer to a wire rack. Peel off the lining paper and leave to cool.

Make the lemon icing. Beat together the icing sugar and lemon juice in a bowl to make a smooth, spoonable icing. If necessary, add a few drops of water or extra lemon juice. Spoon icing over the cake so that it runs down the sides.

RHUBARB CRUMBLE CUPCAKES

Makes 12
Preparation time 20 minutes
  + cooling time
Cooking time 45 minutes–1 hour

sunflower oil, for brushing
275 g (9 oz) young rhubarb,
  trimmed and cut into 1 cm
  (½ inch) lengths

200 g (7 oz) light muscovado sugar
175 g (6 oz) lightly salted butter,
  softened
225 g (7½ oz) self-raising flour
1 teaspoon baking powder
½ teaspoon ground cinnamon
3 eggs
3 tablespoons flaked almonds
icing sugar, for dusting

Line a 12-section muffin tray with paper muffin cases. Lightly brush a foil-lined baking sheet with oil and scatter with the rhubarb. Sprinkle with 25 g (1 oz) of the muscovado sugar and bake in a preheated oven, 200°C (400°F), Gas Mark 6, for 20–30 minutes or until tender and beginning to darken around the edges. Leave to cool. Reduce the oven to 180°C (350°F), Gas Mark 4.

Put a further 150 g (5 oz) of the sugar, 150 g (5 oz) of the butter, 175 g (6 oz) of the flour, the baking powder, cinnamon and eggs in a bowl and beat with a hand-held electric whisk for about a minute until light and creamy. Divide the cake mixture between the paper cases, spreading it fairly level, and top with the rhubarb pieces.

Put the remaining butter and flour in a food processor and process until the mixture resembles coarse breadcrumbs. Add the remaining muscovado sugar and process briefly until mixed. Scatter over the cakes and sprinkle with the almonds.

Bake for 25–30 minutes, until risen and golden. Transfer to a wire rack to cool. Serve dusted with icing sugar.

CHOCOLATE GUINNESS CAKE

Perfect for St Patrick's Day or any other celebration, this decadent cake combines two favourites – velvety Guinness and rich, dark chocolate.

Serves 10
Preparation time 40 minutes
  + standing and chilling time
Cooking time 45–55 minutes

125 g (4 oz) butter, at room temperature
250 g (8 oz) light muscovado sugar
175 g (6 oz) plain flour
50 g (2 oz) cocoa powder
½ teaspoon baking powder

1 teaspoon bicarbonate of soda
3 eggs, beaten
200 ml (7 fl oz) Guinness
25 g (1 oz) white chocolate curls, to decorate
sifted cocoa powder, for dusting

white chocolate frosting
200 ml (7 fl oz) double cream
200 g (7 oz) white chocolate, broken into pieces

Cream the butter and sugar together until pale and creamy. Sift the flour, cocoa, baking powder and bicarbonate of soda into a bowl. Gradually beat in alternate spoonfuls of egg, flour mixture and Guinness until all have been added and the mixture is smooth.

Spoon into a 20 cm (8 inch) spring-form tin, greased and base-lined with oiled greaseproof paper, and spread the surface level. Bake in a preheated oven, 160°C (325°F), Gas Mark 3, for 45–55 minutes until well risen, the top is slightly cracked and a skewer inserted into the centre comes out clean. Leave to cool in the tin for 10 minutes then loosen the edges, turn out on to a wire rack and peel off the paper.

Make the white chocolate frosting. Bring half the cream just to the boil in a small saucepan, then remove from the heat. Add the chocolate, set aside for 10 minutes until melted. Stir then chill for 15 minutes. Whip the remaining cream then whisk in the chocolate cream until thick. Chill for another 15 minutes. Transfer the cake to a serving plate and spoon the chocolate cream over the top. Decorate with chocolate curls and dust with sifted cocoa powder.

INDEX

ACKNOWLEDGEMENTS

Photographs © **Octopus Publishing Group**/Stephen Conroy 20, 22, 33, 37, 43, 84, 104, 111, 114, 130; Will Heap 57, 73, 77, 117; David Munns 54, 58, 70, 87, 123, 139; Lis Parsons 29, 38, 47, 51, 53, 65, 69, 76, 133; William Shaw 11, 12, 16, 18, 27, 28, 30, 44, 48, 61, 66, 74, 88, 91, 92, 95, 96, 103, 107, 112, 113, 124, 128, 129, 134, 136, 140; Ian Wallace 19, 34, 78, 83, 100. **Dreamstime.com**/Jörg Beuge 120; Daniel M. Cisilino 40–41, 108; Danablawrence 80–81; Akadiusz Iwanicki 127; Nataliya Evmenenko 24–5; Evgeny Karandaev 2–3, 4–5; Patryk Kosmider 8–9; Roman Milert 1; Mzumarraga 15; Airi Pung 52; Laschon Hartwig Thomas 3 top right (and throughout); Tiborphotography 118–19; Veronikak 62–3; Ciumas Victor 98–9; Vkuslandia 6.